"The totality of knowledge,
all questions, all answers, reside in a dog."

—FRANZ KAFKA

It's
About

poems *by* Tony Johnston

paintings by Ted Rand

Dogs

HARCOURT, INC.

San Diego   New York   London

Printed in Singapore

For gray wolf, ancestor of all dogs,
and for the dear dogs who have owned me:
Beau
Pedi and Dink
Suzi
—T. J.

For Mary Nelson,
who never met a dog she didn't love
—T. R.

With thanks to Kimi and the groomers at Kimi's Kanine Kastle;
to Dr. Mary Jo Andrews and Dr. Carrie Howes
and everyone at the Foothill Veterinary Clinic for their loving care of Suzi;
and to Midge and Robert Poynter
for their devotion to dogs.
—T. J.

33111 P

Contents

The First Dog

Out of the darkness
the first dog came.
It was as fierce
as the first rain,
as strong as the first wind,
and brave.
Silent as smoke
it moved close
to the fire.
It was faithful
and stayed.

Cave Painting

What story to tell on the stone flank
of forever?
Bison. Bear. Deer. Hawk.
Man. Dog.

A Beagle Speaks of Noses

I should be good.
I wish I could
but
I sniff and sniff.
I catch a whiff
of something new
or old to chew.
What can it be?
My nose drags me
so I drag you.
What can I do
but twine through trees,
check at each pole,
inspect each hole?
Please don't be cross.
My nose is boss.

Little Loaf of Dog

Little loaf of dog, let's go for a walk.
Great tall oaf of man, I intend to balk.
Little loaf of dog, carry you I can.
Great tall oaf of man, that is just my plan.

Dog Biscuits

Dog biscuits, you entice me,
You are shaped so nicely.

The World Is Made of Cookies

The world is made of cookies.
That's what my dog believes.
If I give her one or two,
she heaves sad sighs and grieves
with heartbreak eyes
that tell me,
You're scrimpy. Stingy. Small.
The world is made of cookies.
My dog wants them all.

Spell

It is the eyes.
Dark gypsy jewels, they mesmerize.
Feed me, they plead.
So I do,
just this once.

It is the eyes.
Bold old charms unblinking,
they glow below the tablecloth.
Feed me, they beg.
And I do,
this last time.

It is the eyes.
Spellbinder's dream
boring deep into my heart.
Feed me, they implore,
no sham, no shame.

All resolve dissolves
like cauldron steam.
I give him a treat—
again.

Visit to the Rest Home

Mrs. Jasper is old and thin,
her face finely wrinkled
like an apple too long
in the bin.
Mrs. Jasper is tired.
Stretched.
A skein of cloud
in wind.
Alone,
she gazes at the wall,
dozes now and then
until Duke comes.
When he paws
the bed and shoves
his wet nose
into the old lady's hand,
Mrs. Jasper flutters
awake again.
Her eyes sparkle
like the bold and busy eyes
of a wren.

Guide Dog

FOR BUDDY, THE FIRST SEEING EYE DOG

She's just a plain dog,
black and tan,
a little old,
a little thin,
no special marks,
no special size.
She's just a plain dog.
She's my eyes.

About Cats and Dogs

When it's about cats
it's about magic spells
and sleek and sneak
on windowsills
and spit and spat
and sly and smart.

When it's about dogs
it's about heart.

Shadow

Who knows where the grooming brush
is hidden?
The spot where stolen
loafers lie?
The place old plush toys
go?
And the secret site
of the tennis-ball
burial grounds?
Who knows what pilfered prizes
lurk
in the yards of men?

Shadow knows.

Digging

Digging is a thing I love to do.
Dirt is riddled with old bones to chew.

The News

Rufus brought the paper in,
then lugged it underneath a chair
and stared at it with moon-mad eyes.
He sat on it when I came near.
That very day he ran away.
(He left the paper here for me.)
My eye was caught by one headline,
wreathed with dents from doggy teeth:
GIGANTIC HULL OF MASTODON
DUG UP ON UTAH FOSSIL HUNT
(A photo showed the monster bones.)
I think I know where Rufus went.

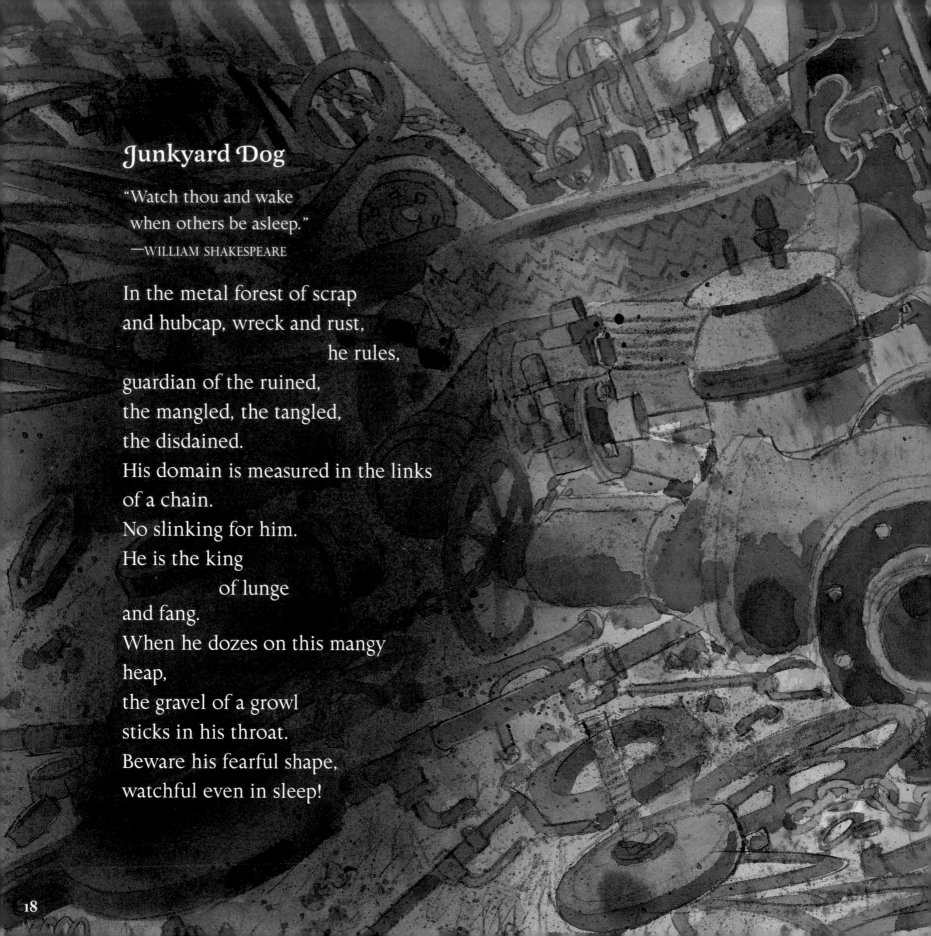

Junkyard Dog

"Watch thou and wake
when others be asleep."
—WILLIAM SHAKESPEARE

In the metal forest of scrap
and hubcap, wreck and rust,
                        he rules,
guardian of the ruined,
the mangled, the tangled,
the disdained.
His domain is measured in the links
of a chain.
No slinking for him.
He is the king
            of lunge
and fang.
When he dozes on this mangy
heap,
the gravel of a growl
sticks in his throat.
Beware his fearful shape,
watchful even in sleep!

Storm

Outside, the night
is drowning.
Lightning sears
the dark.
A tree branch creaks.
Cracks.
Inside, brave Robert
leaps
into my lap.

Woolly Puli

Swish! The mop goes walking.
Who knows how she can see?
By noise or nose or something
extrasensory.

Saint Bernard

The fundamental things that owners need
to know about this canine as a breed
are these: It's quite a job to give a bath.
It slobbers on all objects in its path.

The Groomer

On Saturdays I take Maurice
to get a bath and have all fleas
eliminated from his fur.
(My dog, Maurice, is Pekingese.)

Maurice hates baths on *any* day.
He tries to hide or run away
by chewing through his leather leash.
He never can. He has to stay.

Maurice has teeth like little pins.
His goal in life's to stick them in
the groomer's foot—or failing that,
his knee or nose or chin or shins.

It's Saturday, so in we slog.
The groomer's eyes bulge like a frog's.
(Or like Maurice's.) "*Geez,*" he groans.
"Here come that little bitin' dog."

The Gift

Madame Woo, robed in silk,
                                   roams
her vast domain.
Sometimes she deigns
to sip the milk I leave
with her royal
      lips.
Rippling in ribbons,
the Empress of Disdain
                                   naps
upon her pillow.
On state occasions she *may* bestow
one gift—
the chance for me to hold her on my
                                                  lap.

23

Two Dogs

There were two puppies.
Cockers. Honey colored.
In a basket, huddled
together.
They sucked warm milk.
And slept and slept.
And they got bigger.

There were two puppies
who wrestled socks
and barked at clocks
and nosed beetles
and left puddles.
They ate and ate
and they got fat
together.

There were two puppies
with teeth like needles.
They chewed on chairs.
They chewed their people.
They chewed each other
and they grew to dogs
together.

There were two dogs.
When they took walks,
they ran and ran.
They pulled their people
and smelled the good sweet world.
They pulled and pulled
until one day they were old
together.

There were two old dogs
with grizzled muzzles.
Now and then they nuzzled
each other,
then dozed in the shade
together.

When one dog died
so did the other.

Prayer for the Old Ballplayer

May dog heaven
abound
with tennis balls,
and infinite
angels
to throw them.

Gone

My little dog is gone—
today I used her old bowl
to feed a stray cat.

Old Dog

His memory is dim.
Sometimes when I go out, I find him
napping on my porch mat
in the sun.
He lived here once,
when he was young.
Then his family moved
from town.
He comes back here
to lie down.

New Mother

When the kittens were born,
tiny creatures full of mew
and damp,
their mother sniffed them
once
then wandered off to attend new
matters.
Gilbert heard them
peep.
With his rough tongue
he licked each one,
lifted it,
light as breath,
arranged it with care
in a snug nest,
then settled down
to warm them—
great ungainly
hen.

Bulldog

My dog and my favorite baseball glove
have faces that are similar—
drooping and tough. No glitter.
Could be they're from the same
leathery litter.

Visiting the Vet

My dog is trembling
in the car.
She feels where we are going.
My dog is huddled
by the door,
worn-out with all that knowing.
So I whisper in her ear,
"I am here, girl. I am here."

Mutterly

My dog's name is Mutterly.
He makes my heart melt, butterly.
I love the mongrel utterly.

At the Pound

Eyes bore
        deep
down to the
      soul
speaking
what we cannot
        bear
to know....

PLEASE
DON'T TOUCH

Henry VIII's Dogs

When Henry Tudor was the king,
he loved to feast like anything
on any beast—hart, hare, or boar—
then sling the bones upon the floor.

He gobbled game hens stuffed with sage
and pheasants, hung for forty days
and nights, at least. Then with a roar,
he flung their bones upon the floor.

When Henry's fingers gleamed with grease,
he sucked them (*loudly*, like a beast)
then thumped his fist and screamed for more
bones to dump down on the floor.

While Henry swilled dark ale with malt,
his dogs crouched far below the salt.
Below the table, sooth be known,
awaiting spillage of a bone.

Wolfhound and basset, mastiff, fice,
all slavered, eager for a choice
snippet, when the kingly boor
let slip the bones onto the floor.

In days of Henry Tudor's reign,
bones poured down like heavy rain.
His dogs lay happy at his feet
and hoped he'd never learn to eat.

Pocho Poem

My *perro's* named *Semáforo*,
Traffic Light.
One eye is brown,
the *otro* is as bright
as daytime sky,
not *rojo*,
not one drop.
But when his eyes glow,
everybody
stops.

Found

I found a funny little dog.
Looks like a rat with eyes that bug
and wispy tail. Its ears are sharp.
The main thing it can do is bark
or curl up in my hand to sleep.
(Actually, it's kind of sweet.)
For now, I call him Señor Jack.
I bet somebody wants him back.

I take a pen and paper out,
then start to write a simple note
to set the owner's heart at ease.
(I plan to tack it to a tree.)

An awesome struggle soon ensues:
How can I pass on the good news?
I knit my brow and gnaw my lip.
The pen bends in my anxious grip.
How to perform this golden deed?
How do I spell the foundling's breed?

~~Chiwawaywa. Cheehoohow.~~
~~Chewwuwaha. Chuhwowwow.~~
I try the very best I can,
then write: "Found dog. It's Mexican."

Ron

His name is Ron
and he's a good dog.
When I call, he's there.
Goes everywhere I do, only farther.
Does everything I do, only rougher.
When I growl, he growls tougher.
When I'm sad, he puts his nose
close to my face and just waits.
Ron makes a good pillow;
his fur is plush, like a bear's.
And he doesn't eat much.
Sometimes he licks me.
Ron likes me, but I don't own him.
He comes and goes, like steam.
Never musses my bed, where he sleeps
at night, because he's made up
of light things—
like air, like dreams.

Pet Store

No one looking—
the homeless boy
pats a puppy.

Spill of Moon

Spill of moon
on the bedroom floor—
silver retriever.

The Wonderful Road

He wriggles from Dorothy's
arms
and goes his small bold
                        way,
sniffing
      at scarecrows
and timid
lions,
rushing
      winged
            monkeys,
nipping
      the bony heels
of witches.

Forever this furry
figment
            trots the wonderful
yellow brick road—
                  Toto.

Mr. Lincoln's Doctor's Dog

Mr. Lincoln's doctor's dog
barked for joy and gently wagged
his tail, small flag, when Lincoln neared.
Was this because he liked his beard?
His deep, sad eyes? The jokes he told?
Or for the presidential pat
the dog received the moment that
Lincoln came to visit them,
gangly cricket, tall and thin?
Did *he* know Master's hand could not
heal what war had torn apart—
Mr. Lincoln's wounded heart?
Whatever the reason might have been,
the little corgi loved the man.
He lay beside the bed and cried
the night that Mr. Lincoln died.

Fido

Sleek and black she sleeps
by the fire,
her snores soft
like the breath
of the flames.

Long and long she sleeps
on the hearth
till the logs burn low.

She goes on sleeping,
dark
as the bones
of the fire.

The Old Hound, Dreaming

A fox is on the run! Rejoice!
The old hound, dreaming, once again
lifts his mellifluous voice.

Home for Christmas

Midnight
and the house is breathing
quietly.
Then a screen door creaks.
Outside, feet shuffle.
Whispers rustle
like cold leaves
in cold wind.
Slowly, the dachshund wakes
from her old-dog sleep.
She stiffens at the sounds,
growls,
then snuffles at the crack
below the door,
where, like snow,
a long-ago smell
swirls.
Her small body trembles.
She whimpers with joy.
Oh, my girls! My girls!

At the Manger

She has come a long way,
                    starlight
on her mangy coat
and the dust
of many roads.
She has come a long way,
a clear song
singing in her torn
ears.
She has come a long way
to wait
here in this stable swaddled
with light.

                    Unsleeping
she dives now and then
for a flea
while her wild
gaze roves the hay.
She has come a long way
                    seeking.

45

Curse

May whoever left
the husky tied outside
in the snow,
whoever never plays
with it,
never strokes its fur,
nor speaks
—except to growl
lie down or *stay*—
may he huddle
in the husky's place,
day on day,
night on night,
for company only the pines
and falling snow.
May he know
lonely.

Same Old Story

Old moon rising
white as bone,
old wind sniffing
through a pine,
lone coon climbing
slowly down,
old hound waiting
on the ground.

Same old story.
Same old moon.
Same old hound dog.
Same old coon.

47

Dog

When moon
    drifts
through the dream
of night
and trees and land fall mute,
from his throat a howl
                    lifts
trembling.
                A ghost.
Then he knows this phantom
        voice,
knows a phantom
life.
At moonrise
he remembers he is

                    wolf.

"Visiting the Vet" was first published in *I'm Gonna Tell Mama I Want an Iguana*,
text copyright © 1990 by Tony Johnston, published by G. P. Putnam's Sons.

Library of Congress Cataloging-in-Publication Data
Johnston, Tony, 1942–
It's about dogs/poems by Tony Johnston; paintings by Ted Rand.
p.   cm.
Summary: Presents forty-three poems—some funny, some poignant and philosophical
about dogs and their attributes, including their loyalty to people, their love of food and
smells, and their varied appearances and personalities.
1. Dogs—Juvenile poetry.   2. Children's poetry, American.
[1. Dogs—Poetry.   2. American poetry.]   I. Rand, Ted, ill.   II. Title.
PS3560.O393I77   2000
811'.54—dc21   98-53783
IBSN 0-15-202022-5

First edition
A C E F D B

The illustrations in this book were done in transparent watercolor,
acrylic, felt marker, chalk, pencil, grease pencil, and crayon on mixed surfaces.
The display type was set in Latienne.
The text type was set in Aries.
Color separations by United Graphic Pte. Ltd., Singapore
Printed and bound by Tien Wah Press, Singapore
This book was printed on totally chlorine-free Nymolla Matte Art paper.
Production supervision by Stanley Redfern
Designed by Linda Lockowitz